What is the Bible?

Carolyn Nystrom
ILLUSTRATED BY EIRA REEVES

First published in this edition by
Moody Press in 1994

ISBN: 0–8024–7864–6
Designed and created by
Three's Company, 12 Flitcroft Street,
London WC2H 8DJ
Worldwide co-edition organized and
produced by Angus Hudson Ltd,
Concorde House, Grenville Place,
London NW7 3SA

Printed in Singapore

Moody Press, a ministry of the Moody
Bible Institute, is designed for
education, evangelization, and
edification. If we may assist you in
knowing more about Christ and the
Christian life, please write us without
obligation: Moody Press, c/o MLM,
Chicago, Illinois, 60610.

Do you know about the Bible? I do.

The Bible is God's special Book. It is God's way of talking to me.

Exodus 20:1–17; 32:15–16

But how did God make the Bible?
Once God wrote with His finger on stone. He
wrote the Ten Commandments. Then
God gave those laws to Moses.

God used other people, too. He talked in a quiet voice to the boy Samuel. Samuel said, "Speak, for your servant hears." When Samuel grew up, he wrote in books everything God was telling him. All of Samuel's people knew that God spoke to them through Samuel. His books became part of the Bible.

4

God's Son, Jesus, talked to Paul. Paul took three long trips to tell people far away about Jesus. Then he wrote thirteen books of the Bible so people in those cities wouldn't forget what he taught them.

John 14:25–26

God the Holy Spirit helped four men who loved God remember stories of Jesus' life. They wrote the books called the gospels.

MATTHEW

MARK

LUKE

JOHN

2 Timothy 3:16; 2 Peter 1:20—21

The Bible was written by many different writers, but God showed them all what to write. The Bible is God talking to me—just as He talked to Moses and Samuel and Paul.

Some Bible writers wrote stories of what was happening around them. When I hear those stories it's like traveling to a far-away world of warriors and kings and heroes.

8

Psalm 1; Psalm 119:97–103

Some people wrote the laws of God. The Bible tells me that if I learn and obey those laws, I will be as strong as a tree planted next to water. And I will be happy.

9

Psalm 67

Some wrote beautiful songs. I can sing them when I praise God.

10

Some wrote about happy things and terrible things that will happen some day. But I don't need to be afraid; God will take care of me even then.

Some Bible writers wrote books of teaching. I can study and study, and God will always show me something new about Himself.

12

Many years after those people had finished writing, a group of wise and godly men put all of those books together to form the Bible.

Now I can learn from what they wrote. God gives me His Holy Spirit to help me understand the Bible.

Deuteronomy 30:11–14; Joshua 1:8; Proverbs 6:20–23

God wants me to know His Book so well that words from the Bible come to my mind even when I'm busy with other things.

The Bible is like road signs in a strange town. It tells me what God wants me to do—and not to do.

James 1:22–25; 2 Timothy 2:15

God expects me to know His laws and obey them—just as if they were signs on a road.

Psalm 119:105

The Bible is like a lamp. It helps me see what
God wants me to do.

18

Ephesians 6:17; Hebrews 4:12

The Bible is like a sword. It helps me fight against wrong.

Numbers 23:19

The Bible is true. I can depend on it even when I'm mixed up about everything else.

Isaiah 40:8

And Bible truths will last forever.

1 Peter 1:24–25

I change a lot. I change my mind. I change my clothes. I get dirty. I grow.

Malachi 3:6; Luke 16:1–7

But God never changes. And neither does His Word. I'm glad.

Galatians 1:8–12

Lots of books tell about God, but
the Bible *alone* is God's Word to me.

Many times, evil people tried to destroy all of the Bibles.

Isaiah 40:8

But God always saved a few—for me and you. From those, more copies were made.

Now there are Bibles everywhere:
in stores, in churches,

28

and in my pocket.

You can read the Bible, too.

God wants to talk to you.